A QUEEN'S GROWTH

A New Perspective on Life, Love, and

Relationships

CANDRA JONES

Printed in the United States of America

ISBN 978-0-692-87109-6

Candra Jones Enterprises LLC.

Visit the author's website at

http://www.candrajones.com to order additional copies.

For more information regarding bookings, please email us at info@candrajones.com

TABLE OF CONTENTS

<u>DEDICATION</u>

This book is dedicated to my best friend, my grandfather Junior Lewis. You are the best grandfather and father figure a girl like me could ever ask for. You're an excellent example of a husband and your love for your family is unconditional, and I truly appreciate all that you do.

ACKNOWLEDGEMENTS

Thank you, Lord, for your guidance, unconditional love, favor, and forgiveness.

I want to acknowledge my mother, Crystal, who raised me to be the strong, educated black woman I am today. My spiritual mother, Dr. Ane Mercer, who taught me always to pursue the will of God and to be a faithful servant to the kingdom of God at all times. My godmother, Tracey Carter, who encourages and empowers me to always believe in myself. My aunt, Dr. Vanessa Shannon, who taught me always to stay positive and stay focused. My business mentor and big sister, Dr. Vikki Johnson, who taught me the importance of the bond of sisterhood is that it can never be broken. Thank you all so much for loving me and for all that you do.

<u>INTRODUCTION</u>

What is love? I wonder how many people know the answer to that question. Well in a simple term and brief explanation, everything that happens to us as a human being is an expression of love. Our way of life is an interpretation of what happens us, either positively or negatively. Sometimes, it feels like everything that makes us human is fading away but love changes it all, especially when you are with the right person or you are doing what you love to do, it always feels good. When you fall for someone's personality, everything about them becomes beautiful. The best thing that can ever happen to someone is finding the right person to love. Sometimes, we don't need a calm music, nor a glass of wine but just a moment with the right person, that's what love brings. There comes a time when you meet someone and you will never want to let go of them again for the rest of your life. Once you find that right person or discover that thing that makes you happy in a way that no one else or any other thing can, let it be part of you and never let it go.

Loves on the other side could also be a strong and passionate feeling developed in doing things. We find joy in different things, so obviously, we love doing different things. There always a way to show love to people, either people we love emotionally or people who needs to be shown love. Love answers all things.

Some of the other questions include; who teaches you how to love yourself or how to love others? Where do you go to find the answers? Who am I? What does love and real happiness look like or feel like? Why do we love wrong? What does a healthy relationship consist of? What makes you happy? What is your life's purpose? Do you know the answers to all of these questions?

So let's just lay the truth out there — we as women are taught some crazy things before we come into our journey into womanhood. Like to find a good man who will provide and take care of us and to always be by your man's side no matter what, right? But what if the man we are committed to is not leading and loving us the way we need? Or what if we are raising the men we are dating? Or what if he hasn't found himself yet and is following his homeboys instead of seeking Christ for guidance? We were told to be strong and take care of the household but never taught how to address these issues when dating. Some of these things have shaped our paradigm and have stopped us from receiving the love we truly desire and deserve.

After coming out of a toxic relationship, I found God and started studying his word, reading books, taking courses and building a personal relationship with him. God started opening my eyes and showing me that I had all the wrong ideas and expectations in dating and in life and that's why I kept making the same mistakes over and over again. He started stripping me of guilt, manipulation, self-hate, rejection, fear, pain and abandonment. New GRACE is the best way to describe it. He gave me a dream, a vision, and a purpose and called me to serve his kingdom and that's why you are here today reading my book.

So today I share with you every lesson I've learned, giving you new perspectives on life, love, and relationships.

I grew up in a single-parent household, where love didn't exist, but finances did. My mother was a strong, educated black woman; she always aimed for higher education in every aspect of her life. While raising a child, working a full-time job and pursuing her master's degree, love wasn't on her list of priorities.

I was maybe 6 or 7 when my father passed away of colon cancer, which left my mother alone, which wasn't her choice. I watched my mother work so hard to provide to give me the best life possible that she forgot to love herself or find love for herself and she started abusing alcohol. It led me to believe that a woman doesn't need a man as long as she is strong and a hard worker. But the truth is no woman was created to do it all by herself.

I now sit back in awe of all of the women who raise their kids on their own. I believe as women we automatically abandon our personal pursuits of happiness when we become a parent due to our maternal instinct. Society defines people's happiness through their level of sacrifice and not their obedience. For example, people say things like, "Life is not about you anymore; it's about your children," or "Place your life on hold until your kids are older." Without the love, help or life fulfillment that a woman needs and desires, how can she pour into the lives of others from an empty cup?

I hadn't realized love was such a major concern until I was lost, broken and bitter. By default, I was following my mother's and society's standard of love. I kept getting into toxic relationships without loving myself first or even knowing what to look for when dating, and I had to figure out how and why I was exhibiting these unhealthy behaviors.

CHAPTER ONE

When life gets in the way of living

You are the only thing standing in your way. Being so unsatisfied with myself physically, mentally and emotionally caused me to have bad attitudes and distant relationships and to live in self-hate and doubt. I didn't know how or what to make of this thing called life. I felt like the odds were against me because all my life I had been told by my mother that I was miserable, unhappy and selfish, and that was far from the truth. I just didn't know how to fix it.

(Colossians 3:10) and have put on the new self, which is being renewed in knowledge in the image of its creator.

One day while working at my previous employer, Comcast, my supervisor Lamonte had a sign up on his desk that said "Become the change you want to see in the world," which meant give the world YOU. I couldn't quite rap my mind around it then, but it sounded like if I fix myself first, everything else around me will start to change, and so i did just that. I decided to learn from my pain, give my life to Christ and that I wouldn't allow comfort zones to exist in my world because that means I would be stopping myself and not being obedient to the will of God. I'm crying while I'm writing this. God has brought me such a long way, and I want to do nothing more than live, please and serve him.

I knew that every day my father woke me up with new grace and mercies. I was provided with the new opportunities and blessing he had for my life. I was and still am determined to outsmart my fears and activate and apply my faith. I wasn't going to let my past or my current circumstances dictate the wonderful and abundant life God had prepared for me. It was either purpose and destiny or validation and fear. I chose life and not death. I chose to walk into my destiny with my face beat, hair blowing in the wind and high heels. I was going from pain to purpose and accepting that I was chosen to save my generation.

Dreams of faith

After attending a conference called Saved Girls Rock, I felt renewed, refreshed and restored. A new mind, a new me! Something had shifted, and I didn't know how or what it was. Then God gave me a dream that I was at the Columbus Circle 59th Street train station in New York City and it was crowded and busy. There was a woman in handcuffs with two police officers standing behind her, one on each side. Her face looked as if she had been badly beaten and was bruised. There was blood all over her shirt, and her hair was sticking up on the top of her head, and she was screaming, "He hurt me, he cheated on me and lied to me, he beat me in front of my kids to make himself feel like a man, and I am the who has to pay for it.!" But in front of her lying on a bench hogtied with spots of blood all over his white T-shirt and a glass bottle stuck in his butt was the man who she had loved, trusted and cared for that had hurt her. She looked worse than he did, but from the looks of things, she didn't think that she should be the only one in pain. Get the revelation: Pain ISN'T love, and when a woman is fed up there ain't anything you can do about it.

See, as women, we are taught to be strong because we can birth and carry children. We give too much too soon and end up hurt because we have not discovered our value. The woman in my dream couldn't endure any more pain and decided to seek revenge to hurt him physically the way he had been hurting her mentally and emotionally. In most cases, we retaliate because of the pain when you really should be seeking God for the lesson and the healing.

I used to think being a good woman came with a price until I found God and surrendered my heart to God. Sometimes we as women surrender ourselves to toxic, dysfunctional and emotionally unstable people, and that is not the covenant of God. Instead, we shouldn't accept anything less than the love that Jesus gives to us. Jesus set the standard for unconditional love because he died for your sins.

Don't stay in harmful or unhealthy situations because of loyalty or history, stay in a relationship because it's right. Loyalty can easily become a weakness if you don't know your value and dysfunction can become your habit if you don't know what love it.

In the dream, it seemed as if I were the only person who cared and could hear this woman crying out for help. People were just moving through the train station as if she weren't even there, which sends chills through my body just thinking about it because the world we live in today expects women to be strong and carry everyone else's emotional loads or burdens.

Shortly after that in my dream, the train arrived at the station, and I got on, staring at this broken woman through the glass windows of the uptown 2 train, wondering when and how God was going to use me and if it was my purpose to help broken women find themselves.

Who am I?

When you don't understand the purpose of a thing, abuse becomes inevitable. –Creflo Dollar

Sometimes in life, when you look at things in an overview, you just feel like everything that makes us human is fading away. Especially when you are in a situation you don't deserve to be in. You feel disgruntled about everything that is happening to you. Life has a way of treating us, either in a positive or the other way. The simple fact is that we chose what we want ourselves. Sometimes we do not like the choices we make but what if we don't have any other option? We are all faced with different issues and challenges which are quite different from one another. The ability to unleash the ingenuity in us and face the challenges with an aura of success and victory define us our personalities and makes us who we really are. Every choice we make shapes our fate and every moment we spend is not by our doing but by the grace and opportunity bestowed unto us. What we do in life explains and expresses us and so does our actions echoes in eternity. To be a better person in life, we have to learn to adapt and get over situations. All these things we really make us a better person and set us for the challenges ahead

Have you ever stopped to ask yourself who I am? What is my God-given gift? What is my identity? What is my purpose or divine assignment here on Earth? Who am I called to serve? Sometimes not knowing the answer to these questions will leave you lost and you can end up serving all things no with no purpose. You must search your soul to find the answers.

I remember wanting to be married so that I could cover up my sin because I didn't know who I was or what my purpose was. I thought my sole aim in life was to be somebody's wife. I thought that if I could cover what was happening on the outside, then it would change what I was feeling on the inside. I was lonely, broken and bitter. Listen, ladies: A man can never validate your self-worth or your purpose, only God can. You must know your value, your identity and your creator, to truly know who you are.

I always hear people say things like, "Just graduate high school, go to college and get a degree, get a good job, find a husband and get married and have

some babies and then your life will be complete."
Society suggests these things like you would be
guaranteed happiness if you did all of that. No one
ever taught me or even suggested that I should love
myself first and figure out who I was or my purpose
before doing all of those things. Do not give into the
template of life that was not predestined by God for
your life.

Loving others does not give you an excuse not to
love yourself because the relationship that you have
with God and yourself sets the tone for all your
other relationships in life. You must first SET THE
EXAMPLE. It took me quite some time to realize
that I wanted to be respected but I didn't respect
myself. I wanted to be loved, but I didn't love
myself. I would make jokes about my weight before
others would get a chance because I never thought I
was worthy. Degrading yourself for other people's

humor will lower your self-esteem. Instead, it will destroy your courage to pursue your dreams and love yourself. Finding new ways to love yourself is what's best. Give the world the best example of how you want to be treated by how you treat yourself.

Ask yourself and God these three questions and then fill in the blank:

Who am I?

_____

_____

_____

_____

_____

A QUEEN'S GROWTH

What is my purpose?

_____

_____

_____

_____

_____

Do I love myself RIGHT NOW? (Not past tense)

_____

_____

_____

_____

_____

CHAPTER TWO

If you don't look within, you will go without

Change starts with me

If you constantly claim that you are a victim, then you will always act like a victim. Your mindset is what provokes change. I have been disappointed and hurt by people who I thought loved me, and it caused me to walk around guarded, toxic and broken from pain. I had no expectation level and didn't want to trust people because I had accepted that my happiness didn't matter. I was trying to please people without pleasing God first and myself second. You can be rich in wealth and poor in your spirit; write that down. So always make yourself a priority.

Shopping and doing things for people was sustaining my ego because I needed to feel needed because deep down inside I didn't feel worthy of ANYTHING. I remember thinking that buying something new or going somewhere to be surrounded by people would help me feel less alone in MY OWN SKIN. I thought it would make me feel better about myself.

Let me give you an example: I would call up one of my homegirl Alyssa and tell her, "Let's go the mall, I need something to wear" (like I was going somewhere, lol), and she would respond by saying, "OK, Candra, but you know you don't need anything." We would arrive at the mall and go in almost every store as if there were something new I had never seen online. I would always purchase a bunch of stuff, and my friend would say, "Candra, please put it back; you don't need it." She knew me better than I knew myself at this point. I was shopping to fill voids and to make myself feel worthy of a life that I didn't think I deserved. I hadn't given myself permission to love myself just the way I was. The truth was I wasn't happy with my look or the direction that I saw my life heading, and I was hiding it behind clothes, shoes, and alcohol. I had a lot of stuff that I hadn't even worn yet. I was guarded and hurt, and I was trying to hide it behind material things. I was becoming an emotional spender to try to cover up my pain and secretly I think she knew that I didn't value myself.

Most of the time I would buy things I truly didn't want and end up returning them before the week was OVER. That was something that I had watched my mother do growing up as a child. My mother always loved buying nice things, but she truly couldn't afford them because she had poor spending habits and money management. Her love and value for herself never came from herself, it came from things, and so I followed by an example.

Sometimes most of the things and behaviors that you exhibit today were things that you saw in your childhood. It's time to do some work on the INSIDE!

Write down three things in your life that you struggle with that you learned in your childhood:

1._____

_____

_____

_____

_____

_____

_____

2._____

_____

_____

_____

_____

_____

_____

3._____

_____

_____

_____

_____

_____

Now write down three solutions on how to change them:

1._____

_____

_____

_____

_____

_____

2._____

_____

_____

_____

_____

_____

3._____

_____

_____

_____

_____

_____

_____

Get out of your mind and into your LIFE

And do not be conformed to this world, but be transformed by the renewing of your mind, that you may prove what that good and acceptable and perfect will of God is.

(Romans 12:2) New King James Version

I have always considered myself a happy person. I think it is because God has given me a really BIG heart for people; it has always been my source of light when things seemed dark in my life. Some major road blocks in my life were coming from some of my past experiences, and they were stunning my growth. Was I healing and forgiving my past so I could move forward in my life? Then I started to ask myself, What happens to the wounds left on my body from the pain that caused emotional scarring from unhealed brokenness? These scars come from past relationships where I gave too much of myself, and I lost myself in the process of trying to love someone who didn't even love themselves, or even childhood hurt from a family member where I was too young even to understand what was going on or even a friendship where I trusted someone and they betrayed my trust and lied behind my back.

Let's talk about how these emotional wounds leave scars of hurt, pain, fear, anger, brokenness, shame, guilt, insecurity, low self-esteem, abandonment and manipulation. These emotional scars have left strong feelings that will override our conscious reason, close our minds to other viewpoints and dominate our daily actions if we let them. We cannot walk through life feeling so defeated in our mind that it hinders our actions and responses. Those things created and opened doors in my life for unhealthy, toxic relationships and attachments.

Now, watch this: The negative thought is not the problem; it's what you do with it that is. You will not let these thoughts control you and tell you what to do. You must fight them and not treat them as if they are the gospel. You have to stop self-sabotaging — no more criticism, self-judgment, or comparing yourself to others before anything even happens. Let go of the past. Do not spend time getting attached to what doesn't belong... If you don't own it, then it doesn't belong to you. DON'T CLAIM IT! Your mind is a great storyteller and the most powerful tool you have; know that you are the director of the story and God is the Author and finisher of your fate.

Sometimes accepting the truth about yourself is the hardest thing you can do, but it allows you to release your lies, stand in your power and live in your truth. Understanding why you think and do the things you do is necessary. Check yourself, your mind, your bloodline, your environment, the company you keep (your friends), your priorities and, most importantly, your heart.

Being lost may not always be a bad thing because you must be lost for you to find yourself and allow yourself to be reinvented, renewed and reprogrammed. But always accept and honor where you are at that moment so that you can figure out who you need to become. Embrace the truth about your life so that you can let go of the life that is holding you hostage.

Being authentically you and accepting your truth will always set someone free and bring them healing through your testimony. Break the system and change the cycle.

Let me give you three things that will help you going forth:

Be very mindful of how you feel and what you say. Your mind should always be on the same page as your heart. Focus on your strengths and release any fear or doubt you may have inherited from your past.

Reinvent yourself and be fully aware of your conscious life and less aware of what might be happening in your mind.

Letting go will increase your focus and your quality of relationships and create new possibilities for your future. No more anger, shame, guilt or defeat. You will not let your insecurities or negative self-talk ruin your life. It is time to reinvent, reprogram and replenish yourself.

You have more power than you know

Sometimes our choices and decisions are clear and easy. Often they can be more complicated and it goes without saying sometimes they are extremely difficult! Sometimes we get it right – sometimes we get it wrong. Often we end up feeling somewhere in the middle. Sometimes when we make a bad decision we get a chance to correct it. Logic, data, our feelings and our gut instinct all play an important role in our decision-making process. Trusting ourselves (particularly when it goes against what everyone else is saying) is vitally important. Our power lies in trusting and believing in our choices.

The art of successfully solving problems cannot be done without a crazy determination that knows no failure. "some people are successful because they are destined to be, but many people are successful because they are determined to be. You have 70,000 thoughts a day. How many of them could you possibly be fully aware of? You only use 10% of our brain's capacity. There is so much more power there you have an opportunity to tap into. The Secret and Law of Attraction - tools and pathways to tap into the power of your mind. We are all infinitely connected to a higher source. You create your life from this place - your mind, your beliefs, your thoughts, and what you say.

Be intentional about what you feed your mind (TV, news, and negative conversations), pay attention to your thoughts and words. Notice how your words describe exactly what you're experiencing. It's really the deeper subconscious belief that creates the thought and as you consciously speak it that creates your reality and experience. Not the other way around. It may seem the results - your experiences and circumstances - came first, but it's actually a deeper, buried belief that causes your outer experience.

Deeper beliefs around one's own worth, value, and fear are what the subconscious plays over and over again - in those 70,000 thoughts a day you aren't consciously aware of. Change the deeper beliefs. You must become more aware. Look around, see what isn't working, and pay attention to what you're saying to yourself. Something like "I'm not enough", "It's too hard", "It's impossible", "I'm not safe", "I'll never make it".

"Whether you think you can or can't... you are right." What you speak creates a declaration. Declare what you want even if you don't know how it'll become.

What do you want? Better health, a relationship, more money, better career, more freedom. How do you speak about the things you desire now? To change your circumstances, experiences, and results, pay close attention to your thoughts and words.

Listen to what you say. When you recognize the negative language, change it. It's powerful! Create a mantra or affirmation to repeat to yourself regularly. "I'm enough", "I am safe", "I am loved", "All I need comes to me with effortlessly and with ease."

Say it, feel it, believe it. This process changes the unconscious belief patterns you've created and picked up from others that no longer serves you.

This will transform your life!

Here is a power strategy: Write down three negative

beliefs about yourself:

1._____

_____

_____

_____

_____

_____

_____

2._____

_____

_____

_____

_____

_____

_____

A QUEEN'S GROWTH

3._____

_____

_____

_____

_____

_____

Then say to YOURSELF after each thought, "My mind is having the thought of blah..." You then establish some distance between yourself and that negative thought. Remember if it doesn't belong to you then don't claim it!

CHAPTER THREE

Why do we love wrong?

Someone else's life is not your reality

I watched my mother date, three men, growing up as a child. The first was my father, her husband, who was a hard-working man and passed away, God rest his soul. The other two were grown boys who looked like men, but the truth was she was raising them and me.

In these unhealthy relationships, she was exchanging her strength for their weaknesses, even though there was a lack of love in those situations. My mother was strong, I mean, so strong that it was killing her love life. She was leading; she was the head, She was the provider. She never left a man room to provide, protect or profess his love to her because she simply didn't respect them or see them as real men. She did it all; she looked like a super woman in my eyes.

I later discovered that most women love hard because we were born with an instinct to nurture. But I truly think that loving someone too hard can cause your own self-inflected pain and create desperation. The fears of rejection and abandonment can cause self-hate and cause you to feel like you are not good enough for that person. Don't exhaust yourself for someone who is not even putting in the same effort. The spirit of anxiety or over-excitement sets in where you don't give yourself time to grow into loving one another because your mind his been preprogrammed to what you think your love life should look like. Expectation can sometimes kill intimacy.

The second thing loving too hard can cause you to do is settle for any and everybody. The spirit of desperation and wanting to rescue a man can take over your life because you should never have to lower your standards to be with someone. They should already be on your level or higher. The last two boys I dated wasn't mature enough for me in their life, with their love or in our relationship. I was trying to build a bear, lol. I had watched my mother do that in her relationships, and I had to check myself because I was exhibiting that same behavior in dating. I was trying to prove my love to people who weren't even worthy or capable of receiving it and to add insult to injury I didn't know my value.

So after my self-evaluations, I discovered one of the reasons why I loved wrong was because I was trying to model someone else's life. That was not my reality, and it also wasn't the life that God created for me.

Do you know your worth?

I remember this like it was yesterday. I was 15 years old, and it was a hot summer evening in Jamaica, Queens, New York. My mother and I were going to a cookout that my uncle Curtis was having at his friend's house. Summers in New York were always the best because of the cookouts and block parties.

As soon as we arrived my uncle said he needed to talk to me before we left because he heard from my mother that I thought I was grown because I was turning 16 and I had a boyfriend. He suggested to me that I had lost my everlasting mind and that I am smelling myself. I laugh now because his choice of words tickles me!

So after an hour of being at the cookout my uncle Curtis asked me to take a walk with him. We walked to the front of the house and across the street was this house that looked brand new like no one had ever lived there.

He said to me, "You see that house across the street?" I replied, "Yes." He said, "Tell me what you think about it, and how much do you think it's worth?" I said, "It's nice, and I don't know." He said, "Do you know what's going to happen to the house when somebody moves in that house?" and I replied, "No." He said, "The property value is going to depreciate. The definition of depreciating means to decrease or lose value." I said, "Why, it's so nice?" He said, "Because nothing stays new after it gets used." I didn't know what to say. He then asked me if anyone was living in my house meaning, was I having sex? My facial expression was priceless; I was both puzzled and shocked. He then said

to me, "You better not be having sex or letting any little boys touch on you; you're too young to be taking boys seriously." I didn't understand why he was coming down on me so hard since everybody at my age was having sex already.

At that age, I didn't know anything about my self-worth or value. I didn't know that you should never allow yourself to talk to just any man for attention or that I should never give buyer privileges to renters. Or to know that I should never let my value depreciate, or even that I needed to inspect and evaluate my house after every tenant was trying to move in or was leaving my house.

My grandfather and uncle always said things like, "A man should always earn his keep," and "Nothing worth keeping ever comes easy," and it makes so much since now. The things that are worth keeping are always very VALUABLE.

Sometimes in life, we often settle, or we lower our standards by depreciating our value for someone who can't afford the house, someone who doesn't even deserve a viewing of our house. We get stuck on the outside appearance and forget just because everything looks good on the outside doesn't mean everything is functioning and working on the inside.

We need to know their intentions and plans with our house, but before that, we need to know our value, know who we are and love ourselves so that we will never have to settle or let another human being determine our worth.

So, ladies, you are the house. Courting is viewing the house, The engagement ring is the down payment on the house and when you get married is when your man buys the house, and then you give him the keys. No sex before commitment.

I love you more than I love myself

Journal Entry

07/13/2015

Titled: The incompleteness of a man can create a broken woman

I'm tired of accepting the hurt you keep causing me. I've had enough of being disappointed by your actions and your choice of words. Last night I cried myself to sleep wondering where the man who I love is; I now know that man was just a representative for the man that you have yet to become. We hadn't spoken all day until around 6 p.m. Things are just different, they keep getting worse and you're not acting like who I met in the beginning. I'm waiting for you to appreciate me and see the value of me. I am emotionally drained; I am tired of arguing, I am tired of feeling lonely and misunderstood when I'm supposed to be in a relationship. No more empty promises. Today I have decided to divorce myself from the idea that you are responsible for my happiness. I am going to choose my happiness and me. I cried my last exit tear because you're not worth the pain. There is nothing I can do to fix or go back to because I know I gave my all to someone who wasn't ready. I surrendered my heart to God and asked him to heal me and make me whole again. I refuse to let the person you once portrayed yourself to be, be the reason I let myself keep getting hurt by the person you have now become. The best gift you ever gave me was not just a broken heart for God to heal but a new perspective on relationships and my self-worth.

Are you whole? One of the most common mistakes I see a woman make today is that they are looking for a man to complete them. We as women have been taught to think that when we get a man everything in our life is supposed to get better magically, so we go from one toxic situation to another without healing because we so desperately want to be loved and feel complete. That is mentally and spiritually immature.

God wants all of us in healthy relationships and to experience love, but we must first do the work within ourselves. We must learn to love ourselves before we love others. In my pervious relationships, I truly didn't love myself, which means that I wasn't ready to love or be loved. I was loving through self-hate, pain, insecurity, pride, bitterness, and brokenness. Most people who are broken won't admit it because they like to hide behind their ego, but you can tell through their bitterness and how much they love to complain. Please don't fake your healing because the only person you are hurting is yourself. See, not loving myself caused me to have sex with men who I knew did not love me. Not loving myself caused me to have an abortion when I was 20 years old because I knew I was unfit to raise a child alone. Not loving myself caused me to be in unhealthy relationships to just please people and not myself. Not loving myself was causing me to deny the fact that I had daddy issues. I was constantly lying to others and myself about who I was and what I wanted.

We must understand that loving others should never be an excuse to neglect our self. Pour into yourself what you pour into others. Make yourself a priority in your life; know that you are more than worthy of receiving the love and dedication that you give to others. Believe that and you will receive that — the kind of love that projects confidence and a strong relationship with God that creates value. Love yourself as Jesus loves you. Become completely and totally OK with yourself.

My last relationship taught me so many lessons. One that it's not about how a relationship starts, it's more about what it continuously shows. Second, expecting someone to do what we won't do is not acceptable (Meet the requirements of your requirements.) Three, that dating someone with a lack of maturity or purpose can damage a person who is truly ready for love. Four that we need to be whole and should always deal with our insecurities, abandonment and rejection issues BEFORE we get into a relationship. Lastly, to love ourselves the way that Jesus loves us and never settle for anything less.

Never settle

Always know the difference between what you are getting and what you deserve.

—Candra Jones

I remember my sophomore year in college I dated this DJ because I thought he was so cute and he had swag. I'm cracking up writing this because that's all he had, to be honest. His job was DJing, which meant he never had a steady source of income; I was always paying for things until his next gig came around. All he did was drink and hang out, and that wasn't my thing, but I always followed behind him because I wanted to spend time with him and prove to him that I had his back, although I hated going to clubs because of the way it made my hair smell and people were always spilling their drinks all over my shoes. I was riding for a man who I didn't even believe in. He was always lying to people about his life to boost his ego when we both knew he was broke, and to top it all off he smoked cigarettes, and I had asthma. We did not belong together at all and he was all of the things that I never wanted in a man. I was settling and being complacent because we had physical chemistry. Learn from me, Queens: Don't settle. Just wait because you can't turn a peasant into a king.

Sometimes we settle for what we don't want just because we haven't discovered what we deserve. What do you want in your next relationship? Do you know your worth? What are your requirements or standards? And never apologize for having standards. Understand dating anybody just to have somebody is never going to be fulfilling because you can end up loving the very person whom you despise.

Have realistic expectations for love; don't date to be rescued, date to grow in love.

Standards are your morals, values, and beliefs. Things like what he believes in, his relationship with God. Does he have goals, ambitions? Judge a person from the inside out. Let his character speak for his actions. More than often people fall in love based off of the person's representative and not who they actually are. Knowing your standards makes dating much easier.

Here are some examples of standards:

Man of GOD

Job (He knows his purpose in life)

Car (transportation)

His own place (stability)

Good relationship with his mother and father (foundation)

He has a vision/goals and dreams (ambitious and can bring something to the table)

He loves himself (self-worth)

Family-oriented

Has a big heart

Wants kids

Always keep your standards but compromise your preferences. Looks mean nothing to an empty soul. Everything needs a firm foundation for you to build from. You should never date someone without the prerequisites because they won't be eligible to take your class.

Meet the requirements of your requirements

Have you become the love you want to attract?

We only attract what we are ready for. For example: If you want a hard-working, God-fearing, ambitious, loyal, wealthy man, you must first be that girl. The man you marry represents you, and you represent him.

God made Eve from Adam's rib, which means she was already a part of him, but most importantly,

Adam knew who he was and his responsibility to God. He had a job, and that was to name the animals. After he had done God's work, God said, "It is not good for man to be alone, so I will make him a helpmate." Adam was not lazy, and he didn't complain because he was complete and whole. It is not enough to just think highly of yourself and not put in any work. We must grow, heal and learn from our past experiences. We must be the love that we want to attract. For all of my single ladies, God has the perfect man for you, with all of the qualities of Adam and then some, but you must work while you wait and become the best version of yourself. When Boaz saw Ruth, she was gleaning in the fields, working on herself. While you wait to enhance your prayer life, exercise, work on your purpose, strive for excellence in every aspect of your life. Get a clear understanding of your identity before you become one flesh with someone else.

Love like you've never been hurt: Love is letting go of fear

I remember the time I tried getting into a new relationship after not being over my ex. I was dating but still having side conversations with my girls about my ex and all the things he did wrong while trying to talk a new guy. I was programming my mind to do two things: One, become a victim, and two, make my future pay for my pain. I felt like I lost so much but truthfully I wasn't allowing myself to heal and I wasn't ready to love like I have never been hurt before. So many times we as humans have the tendency to carry our old issues, problems and baggage into a new relationship.

I love having thought-provoking conversations with women who say they want a husband but don't believe in love or either block every man who is trying to talk to them. I like to ask questions like these: How is true love going to find you? Why does every man have to go through the wilderness to get to your heart? Do you know that your past doesn't determine your future? Did your pain create a blueprint for what you won't allow? How do you know if every man is out to break your heart?

Healing before dealing allows you to have a fresh start and a new beginning, to not live your future through your past but to believe in love again.

Please understand that you will not be happy in any situation if you are still holding on to your past.

We must allow ourselves time to heal, forgive and forget the things that caused us the most unbearable pain and learn from it so we can become the best versions of ourselves. Here are three things we must do to love like we have never been hurt:

Find out what real love is

Ask God to heal your heart — make that your prayer.

Get understanding because pain is not love.

Being a good thing means you don't audition; it means you're in position

(Proverbs 18:22) He who finds a wife finds what is good and receives favor from the LORD.

My ex and I were dating for at least two months when I started hearing stories about his ex. We were just dating and getting to know each other and he would express all these horrible things that his ex had done as if he was the only angel on earth and she was a devil in disguised (warning sign). That's a sign of a grown boy and also a man who is toxic and not healed.(PSA: Men take reasonability for there actions) He told me those things because he wanted my sympathy and to lower my standards and because he was putting me to the test. Over time I started losing myself trying to make him whole because of all of the sad stories he told me. I was trying to prove to him my love was real and that I wasn't her. I would buy him small gifts, tolerate his unhealthy lifestyle and believe in his lies because I felt he was dealt an unfair card in his previous relationship, but I had to realize that was never my debt to pay and what you do with your pain is a choice. His ego was being stroked and my self-esteem was being shattered. It was all mind games; always remember there are three sides to a story and we only go through what we allow.

He was acting like a victim and I was falling for it just so he could feel better about his self. I honestly felt bad for him and I wanted to fix him with my love because I thought he had potential. All dogs have potential — that's why we rescue them, lol.

See, but what I didn't know was that being a good thing is never tied to loving a broken man and trying to make him whole. That's not your job and that's the quickest way to lose yourself. Being a good thing is not about receiving acceptance or approval from a man that you're worthy of being loved or even being his wife. Being a good thing is not about dating a grown boy and giving him husband privileges.

Being a good thing is about being a Queen. A queen doesn't need audition to be a man's helpmate; she has already been pre-approved by her creator, she just needs to be in position and never lower her standards.

God put Adam to sleep and took one of his ribs and turned it into Eve (his wife), bone of his bone, flesh of his flesh. She never had to audition to be in his life. She just needed to be in position. She didn't have to raise Adam into the man she needed him to be because god had already taken care of that. She just needed to understand her role.

Understand when a man of God is serious about you being his wife and he knows that you are a good thing he will not play any games with you because he knows how to please god and that his favor is attached to the women that he chooses. The most important thing about being a good thing is being whole and knowing your value. Be a rib and not a door mat.

CHAPTER FOUR

What daddy never told his little girl

Men always want to be a woman's first love. Women like to be a man's last romance.

—Oscar Wilde

A man must earn his place in your life

Last year I met a man who I thought was going to be my husband. He was sweet, handsome, compassionate and a gifted writer, but he just wasn't ready. He hadn't found himself in God yet and didn't know who he was or even how to love himself.. Our unhealthy relationship was tearing me apart because I was constantly trying to prove to him that he was worthy of me while decreasing my own value. I had my mind made up and I was tired of dating. Without anybody's consent I started acting like his wife. I was OK with functioning as a wife in my mind and I thought it was a big accomplishment. Plus I just wanted to have one of those relationships that I saw on TV, but that wasn't my reality and there was one thing missing… he never asked me to marry him lol I was trying to play house and make him my ken doll and it blew up in my face. He told me out of his own mouth that I was giving too much, and I was moving too fast. I then realized that I was trying to Wife him.

I realized that treating a man like a husband will not make him see the wife in you. All a man needs to see is that your are loyal, responsible and loving — that's it!

Don't over do it.

Here are three lessons that I learned from this situation:

Don't Wife a man… you taking him out to eat, you paying all of his bills, you cooking and cleaning for him. Just so he can call you wifey and never actually put a ring on your finger.

Just be a good thing. Proverbs 18:22 says, "He who finds a wife finds a good thing and obtains favor from the LORD." Queens, before you can become a wife you must be A GOOD THING! What is that? Something worth KEEPING! Be completely content with yourself and be his friend first.

Let the man earn you. You cannot give it all away because you're lonely and you want the relationships that other people have. He must find you and you cannot choose HIM. He must want to make you his WIFE because he knows you're an asset to the kingdom of God. You are worthy to be found.

Choosing a man based on the assumption that you could fix him or rescue him like some dog and dress him like he is some Ken doll will never work because once you start to feel bad for him or pity him and start treating him like a child, you will lose respect for the man on the outside and save the boy who is crying wolf on the inside. And just that fast your PROSPECT then becomes your PROJECT. He has to make the decision to grow up, and if you can't love him the way he is then cut him off and turn him over to God. You must let him go so he can grow. A man must have discipline, integrity and responsibility in order to be your husband. There are rules to everything we do in life.

He just wasn't ready

If a man is not concerned about keeping you happy, you are not a priority in his life and he might not be ready for the kind of commitment you need. The things that mean the most to us in life, we work hard to obtain. In the last days when my ex and I were talking he shared something with me that I will never forget. First thing was that he knew he didn't deserve me and secondly that all men know better even if they tell you they don't. To me it meant that all men know the difference between a king and fool, a boy and a man, potential and purpose.

I believe God created man with the intuition to be a real man but some men struggle with identifying it because of their past insecurities, brokenness, selfishness and lack of self-esteem. They're afraid

76

of love because it requires vulnerability and reasonability. A man has to find his own ambition and reasoning to love, no more rehabilitation. So please understand this: If a man walks out of your life that means that he simply wasn't ready for love and doesn't deserve to be in your life. It's not personal; he is still trying to figure out who he is. Most men are explorers, and until they are certain that they are stable or mature enough they will not take love seriously.

My grandfather always says to me a man must be sure of his self before he can truly consider himself a man. His finances, self-esteem, relationships and life must have order. He must understand his role, responsibility and priorities. Don't ever make excuses for a man because it gives them a reason not to show up or show you the man that they claim to be. Men handle business, but boys make excuses.

(We will discuss more of that later.) Remember, a man must earn his place in your life. Actions over words in my book; let his character speak for his actions. Let them know I can't hear you; I need you to show me. Trust me, it works, because real men don't have a problem proving themselves. They like to feel needed — it strokes their ego.

Men aren't afraid of responsibility but boys are because they are not sure of themselves. A man who truly loves you will provide, protect and profess his love for you. A man who truly loves you will lay down his pride and ego for you. A man who truly loves you will change for you; you don't have to convince him to change because he's willing to make them change. There are seven major principles that a man should have to be considered a man of great stature. Check the man that you are currently dating to see if he has these things:

Faith

Responsibility

Stability

Integrity

Character

Purpose

Vision

Let go or be dragged

The root of all suffering is attachment. —Buddha

Most of the time we force ourselves to love people or to be in unhealthy relationships because of our attachment to a person. It's only because of our past or known history that we feel stuck or undeserving. You must understand this: Love is not war and just because you started with them doesn't mean you must finish with them. Be loyal to what feels right. Hurt people hurt people and sad people make people sad. Don't expect him to be real with you if he's not real with himself. Ladies, if you meet a man who is broken and dealing with past hurt, issues and insecurities and doesn't want to grow then you let him GO. It's not your job to fix someone who is broken or lost. We should always hold people accountable for their actions. When dating or in a relationship both parties should come into the relationship whole, knowing who they are and what the intention is for the relationship. You can't change a man; a man has to want to change to be with you.

You can love someone but only God can fix them, and the reason why I know this is because I myself ended up broken and lost trying to heal a man's past hurt and pain.

I let loneliness turn into lust. Desperation started to sink in. I was tired of being alone but afraid of being hurt, so I accepted anybody just because my mind was ready to settle down and be with one person for the rest of my life, even though my heart was unsure and I didn't know how valuable I was.

So the minute you meet someone you begin the infatuation process and you start finding ways to change him and dress them like he's your baby doll. That is a clear indication that he is not the man for you, but yet you are willing to settle. You are falling in love with his POTENTIAL not who he actually is. By doing so you will affirm his insecurities of him thinking he wasn't good enough for you in the first place and also stroke your own ego by making him your project instead of your prospect. Don't ever feel bad for making a decision about your own life that upsets other people. You are not responsible for their happiness. Anyone who wants you to live in misery for their happiness should not be in your life to begin with because that means they have a hidden agenda. Consider the break up as a blessing.

Project vs. Prospect

You think he has potential but he needs to know his purpose. —Candra Jones

Have you ever dated a guy and thought there was a couple things about him that you could change? Some things that you didn't like? Maybe his career, his work ethic or his circle of friends? You started wanting to dress him. You started checking him about his friends. You started questioning him about how he spends his money and how he should act as a man. Ladies, he just went from being your prospect to your project in a matter of seconds. Instead of loving him, you wanted to fix him. Your EGO just stepped in and took over and you started dating him based off of his potential and not his purpose. I bet you want to know why? It's because you didn't see him as a man, you saw him as a boy, so you wanted to raise him. As a woman, it is your natural instinct to nurture and help anybody, but you have to all use your discernment.

I once dated this guy and the only thing I could say I liked was his teeth and that he had a nice smile. How shallow was that. I never said I admired his work ethic or his confidence or even how he loved God. I saw him as a follower and not a leader. I just liked his looks. He was broke, busted and disgusted. I truly saw him as a project because deep down inside I didn't think he was man enough for me because he wasn't sure of himself. It seemed like he didn't know who he was or what his purpose was so therefore I started treating him like my Ken doll, instead of loving him the way he was or even walking away from him. I decided that I had enough finances, love, support and loyalty to make him whole. To make him see the man who was buried inside of the grown boy's body. I was sadly mistaken.

We as women were born to nurture but we have to be careful when dating. The person you date should be your equal if not more. Do not date on the level of your esteem; you date above that because a real man wants to see you happy and not stressed.

There are three things that you should never do when dating a man:

Try to force yourself to love him, when you are unhappy or you don't love yourself. It will lead to future disappointment and resentment.

Pity a man. Why? Because you will lose respect for him, which creates a lack of trust. A man is supposed to be the head, the leader of his household. If you don't respect his decisions then how can you trust him with your life?

Try to fix a man. I'm sorry ladies let me be real, K. Michelle said it best: "You can't raise a man." It is never your job to fix a man. Every human being needs to be held accountable for his or her thoughts, feelings and actions. You can influence them to be better but you can't change them.

When you're dating always question: Is he a prospect or a PROJECT?

Grown boys

If he can't lead you, he can't love you. —Candra Jones

It was 4th of July and my ex and I were up arguing all night on the phone because he was supposed to come visit me for the holiday but instead he chose to go some cookouts with his friends. There I was, five months into a long-distance relationship bawling my eyes out over a grown boy because he wasn't acting like the man I fell in love with. In the beginning he said all the right things, told me everything I wanted to hear.

I was so mad, upset and hurt because his actions weren't adding up to his words. This wasn't the first time he had lied or made up a story; this was starting to become a pattern in our relationship. Next thing you know I was crying like someone had stolen my dog because I didn't accept his lies, his games or his doggish ways. I remember him saying, "Candra, I'm sorry. What do you want me to do?" over and over and I couldn't even respond, all I could do is cry. I was broken and tired of the arguing, fighting and complaining. All I wanted was for him to show me the man he said he was. Not even realizing I fell in love with his representative. I fell in love with a grown boy; he was just a boy pretending to be a man. How do I know? Because an actor can't act forever, eventually they will have to take their masks off, and when they do reality sets in. A grown man is accountable for his actions and accepts responsibility effortlessly because he knows that's what life is about — taking care of your priorities first.

A grown boy always has a representative. He is an insecure little boy who doesn't know how to be a man, who hides behind his ego and lies while utilizing manipulation tactics to make himself seem greater than what he truly is, instead of looking inward to man up. Queens, that is what you call a GROWN BOY aka Jody! By definition a grown boy is a boy trapped on the inside of a man's body. You cannot raise a man but you can influence him to better. Every man has free will and the power to change. Do not make excuses for a man because of sympathy. He then becomes toxic and complacent; and he will never forgive and forget his past. Too many men get away with faking who they are instead of growing into their true potential because of the women in their life.

Signs that you have or are currently dating a grown boy

Does not take accountability for anything that happens in his life. He lies about everything, makes excuses instead of taking accountability and always want to argue. Excuses and lies are his favorite game.

Seeks highly ambitious women so he can lower their standards because he is toxic and likes manipulation and control.

Loves to discuss the random women he has or is currently sleeping with like they are objects with his homeboys to protect his ego and hide his insecurities and low self-esteem. Puts women to the test to see what they can do for him.

He pretends to be hard, cocky or arrogant and truly has nothing going on in his life! He needs constant reassurance. He lives life always trying to boost his ego especially in the presence of other men.

 Doesn't know who he is yet: He lacks purpose, motivation and drive and does not know what to do with his life, so he lives a bitter, toxic and unhealthy life.

He doesn't respect the will of God. He fills voids by drinking, partying and smoking to fix his past pain instead of dealing with it.

Lesson: if a man cannot be honest with you if he is not honest with himself.

Signs and red flags

My previous relationship was so toxic that every time we argued he showed me a different side of him aka red flag and I would ignore them. One day my ex and I got into an argument over his ex-girlfriend texting my phone. She stated that he was a good guy, that they were supposed to be getting back together and she hurt him and that he deserved to be with someone who made him happy although she still cared about him. How twisted was that? He told me some of the story; he just didn't tell me about them getting back together. I truly believe they were bonded together by a soul tie. They were in a long, four-year, emotionally unhealthy relationship and they had unresolved issues and were both adults acting like childern. They were only separated for a couple of months. They needed time to find themselves again before they entered into another relationship.

See, that was a red flag right there and I over looked it. Oh, but it gets better. So a couple months down the line in our relationship my ex would say things like "I don't deserve you" or "You are just too good to be true." He would even ignore my feelings about things I considered to be disrespectful. Ladies, please read between the lines. If the man you are dating is showing you red flags or signs of toxic behavior he just isn't the man for you and you deserve better. Accept it and move on. We must stop trying to make people be who we want them to be instead of who they truly are just because we are afraid of losing them. Take the RISK because all men know better even if they don't admit it. My ex showed a lot of toxic behaviors and those were immediate signs that the level of commitment that I was giving was not going to be reciprocated. How can you give someone love if they don't believe in love? How can you be honest with someone if you're not being honest with yourself?

There were times when we would have disagreements and would never come to a resolution due to the fact that he never liked to resolve our issues, he just kept wanting to sweep them under the rug. That is a red flag right there. How can you have a relationship without communication? (And text messages are not considered communication if you were wondering.) Adults communicate.

Now it is possible to love someone and they change, but they have to change for themselves and not for you because if things don't work in their favor they will end up resenting you. They have to acknowledge the problem in order to fix it and that takes maturity and responsibility. But I want to give you some signs and red flags that we miss in relationships.

Lack of communication: Lack of communicating leads to unresolved issues. Not being able to express your feelings openly creates emotional distance in some relationships. We should never leave partners to have to deal with a situation on their own. Saying whatever to the situation or giving the silent treatment is simply not an option.

Non-resolution of past relationships: Not just in intimate relationships but also with family and friends. If one hasn't learned to take responsibility for their actions and is unable to evaluate why past relationships haven't worked out, or consistently blames others for all of their problems, you can bet a million dollars that the same is going to happen with your relationship.

Feeling insecure in the relationship: This is huge for women. "Indecision is decision." Not knowing where you stand with someone in a relationship is a problem. Don't just build on physical connections or temporary moments of happiness. You should never feel uncertain, uncomfortable or anxious about where your relationship is heading because you will start to seek reassurance or validation from your partner. As a result, you may be working overtime to keep your relationship intact while your partner makes little to minimal effort.

Lack of trust: When a person has difficultly being honest with themselves, it may hard for them to be honest with you. See, a lot of this behavior may not be calculated and malicious but simply a learned way or habit of coping. Please understand that a lie is still a lie whether there is reasoning behind it or not. A person who doesn't hold himself or herself accountable for their actions lacks integrity and will always lack respect for their partner. If there always seems to be a missing piece of the puzzle, it normally is; trust your intuition.

Irresponsible, immature and unpredictable: Some people may have trouble mastering the basic skills in life, such as having healthy relationships, managing their finances, making plans for their life and their future. If they state they are still trying to find themselves, they still may be working on growing up.

Controlling or abusive behavior: Any form of abuse such as emotional, physical, verbal, psychological and certainly physical. Someone who will try to divide and conquer every relationship in your life. They may want to control who you talk to and the direction of your life. They will limit your life to what they believe only. This is a huge sign of insecurity.

Your friends and family don't like your partner: See, when you're in a relationship you can't see how it looks on the outside, you can only see what's going on in the inside. We all need a second pair of eyes and often times our family and friends believe that we deserve better than we are receiving. They only want the best for us.

CHAPTER FIVE

He can hold you, but can he handle you?

The moment we want to believe something, we suddenly see all the arguments for it, and become blind to the arguments against it. Sometimes love blinds us, other times it lets us see.

—George Bernard Shaw

When a man really wants you

See, when a man really wants you, he will do whatever it takes to get you and keep you because he understands that you are an asset to his life and not a liability. A man will only act right for the woman he truly wants to be with. He understands the principle of making a good woman his wife. He will listen to the voice deep within him that says, she's a winner.

But listen, ladies: A man can only treat you like a queen if he sees himself as a king. I'm going to be completely honest with you when a man decides he is ready to start building his future he takes his love life seriously. He doesn't just date to mess around; he dates to find a wife. There won't be any mind games, lies or unhealthy behaviors. (Notice I said man and not a boy) He will want to let the world know that you are his. Steve Harvey breaks it down into three simple steps: Protect Provide and Profess. This is how you know if a man is serious about you especially if you are in the dating stage. In the book of Genesis God put Adam into a deep sleep and took a rib out of his body to create Eve, and immediately Adam claimed her, and he named her. So no matter how good you cook, no matter how good you look, no matter how many followers you have on Facebook or Instagram, if a man wants you, you will know. But some of us women are trying to be a rib to a man who is still SLEEP. When a man doesn't choose you that is perfectly OK because that just means you deserve better and he wasn't your king. If he is hiding you, he is trying to keep his options open or avoid being hurt or vulnerable. The only things that can make a man be faithful are self-control and the fear of God. Don't get into a relationship because you're lonely get into a relationship because you're READY, and we must stop submitting to men who don't know how to lead.

Recently one of my childhood crushes contacted me, and we were talking and getting to know each other again, and I asked him some questions to see if he was somebody who I would want to grow with. I cut straight to the chase; my time is precious, and I don't want to waste it. I asked him these four questions, and he failed the most important one. HIS faith. He said he doesn't do church or GOD. That was a deal breaker. So I cut him off immediately. Know what you're looking for in your helpmate so that you never settle.

Ladies, always ask a man these four questions when dating:

What are your goals in life? Short/long term. Do you have a plan, purpose and a model for your life?

What are your religious beliefs? Your faith?

How do you feel about marriage and kids?

Can you envision me in your future?

Get these questions answered in the beginning rather than waiting after the breakup, guessing and forcing your beliefs on him. You won't have wasted any of your time, and you will know whether he's a match for you, and his words should always follow his actions.

Dear Queens, don't just settle for dust

There are going to be times when you want to fill the void of loneliness by revisiting the past. Don't…Don't go lurking and checking their social media, talking with their friends and family or even responding to their messages. Instead turn to God and pray for peace, discernment, love, wisdom and guidance. There will be times where you are going to question yourself; you're going to replay in your mind the happy moments you had, forcing yourself into denial. It's not your heart — it's your ego playing tricks on you. Don't allow your mind to think something that your heart can't feel; if he doesn't do his part, he doesn't deserve your heart. Understand that this relationship or situation did not break you, it only made you wiser, stronger and more beautiful, but Queen, please learn from this experience because everything in life has a lesson and a blessing attached to it. Understand everything you go through will grow you, and your new strength will become your confidence.

Let me remind you that you are a queen and queens don't lower their standards, they only raise them, and they are not victims they are victors. Your self-worth should always come before your relationships. You may be afraid to date, love or even be open to another man that do not be dismayed; God will make you whole again and heal your heart. God never stops loving you no matter what you go through. ; it You have more years ahead of you than behind you, so let go and let God. The breakup was a blessing in disguise.

I urge you to forgive them and forgive yourself because forgiveness is the key to healing. Forgiveness is for you and not for them; do not look for a replacement to fill what you lost. If you didn't know, love didn't hurt you; somebody who didn't know how to love hurt you. And understand you can't grow old with a guy who refuses to grow up.

So now I want you to focus on YOU. Focus on your goals and rebuild your life. Love yourself like you never loved before, believe in yourself and seek God, and trust me, the right man will find you.

Never take your crown off because you are the daughter of a king.

Prayer for Discernment

Thank You, Father, for your great love for me and that you know my need and the paths that I will take in the future. Help me to discern what my future needs are in life, love, and relationships and not to confuse them with my fleshly desires or the vanities of my heart.

Lord my heart is open to your leading, guidance, and wisdom – and my desire is that I do only those things that are righteous in your sight. Father God, I pray that I may be quite to listen to your voice and slow to assume that I know your will when it is my fleshly thinking. I pray for insight and direction in every situation in my life. I pray that you renew, restore or rebuild my life and keep me in perfect peace as long as I keep my mind stayed on you.

Lord, I know that your ways are inscrutable and your mind is unknowable and you said that if a man lacks wisdom, they should ask God, who gives generously to all without finding fault, and it will be given to them. So I want to thank you advance for governing and directing my steps in Jesus name I pray, Amen!

CHAPTER SIX

Let them go so you can grow

Recently a young lady came up to me and said, "I don't trust men. How can I learn to trust men?" and my answer was forgiveness. Forgiveness is a gift that you give to yourself that releases hate, hurt, pain, anger, and bitterness, so you can make room for what belongs in your life. You cannot receive your next blessing or breakthrough in your life if there is no vacancy available for it. Operating from a place of unforgiveness can cost you some relationships and also put limitations on your life.

See, most of us don't want to forgive people because it gives us an excuse or reason to blame others for our self-inflicted pain. Forgiveness gives you peace of mind and keeps you from hindering yourself. We have been taught that it's OK to walk around angry and that pain is love, and it's NOT. Love doesn't hurt people; hurt people, hurt people because they haven't forgiven and they have hurt in their heart.

If you don't forgive yourself, you will start to feel bitter, unhappy and unworthy.

Forgiving yourself and someone who hurt you frees you of dead weight, no matter the time frame, and please understand forgiving them doesn't mean you will forget it, it just means you won't remind them of it.

If you're currently dating and you have forgiven your partner over and over, chance after chance, then they are taking your forgiveness for granted. Grace is forgiveness being taken for granted. Cut them off completely because they simply do not deserve your LOVE.

If you can't forgive someone you might have to forget him or her. Just because you love them doesn't mean they need to be in your life. Two unhealthy, un-whole, toxic people do not belong together because all they will do is try to continuously hurt each other. But if you choose to forgive someone in your life you cannot bring up the past, you must leave the past in the past and build a new foundation for your future, and this must be a mutual decision between both people. Forgive yourself and them and then turn them over to God.

Here are five reasons why we need forgiveness:

Unforgiveness will block your blessings and stop you from receiving the love you truly want.

You can become the person who hurt you by reliving your pain...you will turn into a victim.

It will create pride and anger, keep you close-minded, bitter and afraid of rejection. You will become toxic and judgmental, and truthfully this is the plan of the enemy to keep you living an unhappy life.

It is a waste of time. You have more years ahead of you than behind you; focus on your future and not your past.

God forgives us daily.

Right now I want you to write down the name of the last three people who hurt you and forgive them. Say, "I forgive you and my past will not hinder my future."

1._____

_____

_____

_____

2._____

_____

_____

_____

3._____

_____

_____

_____

_____

Then forgive yourself for three things:

1._____

_____

_____

_____

_____

2._____

_____

_____

_____

_____

3._____

_____

_____

Breaking soul ties

Have you ever dated someone and you guys keeping getting back together? Do you keep messing around even though you don't trust each other? You guys hook up when it's convenient even though you weren't in a committed relationship? Do you want to have sex with the person? Ever date someone and feel like you just can't get over them?

I know the feeling all too well. Once my ex and I had broken up I wanted to revisit my past, and I couldn't understand why. I thought things like, Maybe he was meant to be my husband, or maybe I

114

just need to give him a second chance because I was too hard on him. But the truth was that I had a soul tie to him. Our souls were knit together through intercourse, and no, he wasn't my husband. Sometimes we use familiarity to hide the fact that we're afraid to move on with our lives and see what God has in store for us.

See, a soul tie can serve many functions, but mainly it's when two souls join and become one flesh. This is why sex is sacred and should be done only in marriage because every person that you have sex with you take a piece of them with you. Soul ties can draw you to someone who is manipulative and has controlling ways and will make you believe they love you even though they treat you like dirt. You won't understand what's going on and you will keep allowing it to happen. Know the difference between love and lust.

Although you can't see your soul, it goes where you go. So when you lay down with a man, and you give him your body, your souls connect. Soul ties are formed through sexual and close relationships. In order to break the soul tie, you must first repent of all your sins. Secondly, forgive them and yourself. Thirdly, remove and give away and physical evidence of your relationship. Keeping those things in your house will remind you of the relationship does nothing for your future. Lastly, pay attention to your heart and the words that come out of your mouth. You don't want to start cursing your life because of hurt and pain. Having things in common with someone doesn't make them your soul mate.

Heal and be made whole

(Psalms 51:10) Create in me a clean heart, O God, and renew a right spirit within me.

When my last relationship ended for good, I was broken and depressed. I didn't want to accept the fact that I had invested my time, my money and my heart into someone who wasn't who they said they were. I wanted closure and answers, fast. Listen, Queens, the answer to your questions is already inside of you, and there are some voids that only God can fill. It's time to acknowledge your faults and ask God to heal your pain, and healing takes time, so don't expect it to happen overnight.

Holding on to pain only hinders you from receiving and attracting what you truly want in your life. Pain will change your perspective on your beliefs, your reactions to people and life itself. So don't be bitter, be BETTER. We must identify the things that hurt us in order for us to heal. Do not get into a new relationship without solving the issues inside of you because your past doesn't belong in your future. Now write down three to five things that have hurt you (pain points), and then cast them on Jesus. Use them to free someone else by sharing your testimony of how you overcame that particular situation.

Here are 5 steps that you should use for healing:

1. Seek God, read and study your Bible or seek wise council

2. Gain new wisdom and get an understanding of why you went through what you went through. Try to figure out what God was trying to show you and what you need to work on.

3. Find your purpose and figure out what you want out of your life.

4. Love yourself. Find out what truly makes you happy and who you truly are.

5. Become the love you want to attract. If you're single, focus on becoming the mate that you desire.

CHAPTER SEVEN

Affirmations for Queens

As a queen, it is import to have positive self-talk. What you speak out of your mouth is connected to how you feel. Changing your self-talk will help you stop questioning and doubting yourself. It will increase your faith and your esteem. Whatever you speak over yourself is what will manifest in your life. You have to think about yourself the way God thinks about you. You have to renew and transform your mind to believe that God made us in HIS image. You must believe that you are loved, that you are beautiful, that you are gifted, that you are blessed, that you are prosperous, that you are whole.

A QUEEN'S GROWTH

Repeat these affirmations to yourself daily:

*I am a queen

*I am beautiful

*I deserve more

*I am worth more

*I will not settle for less than God's best

*I love myself, and every day I will prove to myself that I love myself

*I am fearfully and wonderfully made by God

*I am blessed

*I prosperous

* I am successful

* I am healed

* I am whole

* I am and will always be loved by God

* I am the daughter of a KING

Takeaways

In closing here are some things I want you to know about life, love, and relationships.

1. No investment before commitment: No sex before marriage, no friends with benefits, no "situation ships." Giving your mind and body to someone who doesn't see the value in you is like selling your soul to the devil. Marriage is where you get the benefits package, and if cannot wait until marriage wait at least 90 days. No job gives its employees benefits without a 90-day probationary period. During this timeframe, you should be dating

and getting to know each other, and he should be courting you, wowing you and showing you his true character. Don't let a man come and set up shop and get you to lower your standards. Build your relationship on a stern foundation, a foundation that is built to last. And don't worry about his feelings because anything worth working for is worth keeping. Let the man chase you, build up his expectation. If a man can't wait 90 days, you won't have to cut him off because his actions will show it...

2. Heal before you deal: Learn to forgive and let go! Your past will never determine your future. Do not hold on to any pain or hurt because most people aren't even taught to love themselves. So forgive them and forgive yourself.

3. Never give more than the title permits: Always date with a purpose (intention). Know exactly what you are getting into. Always ask questions and get to know the person before you have sex because sex makes you fall for potential and not actual actions. Protect your heart. A boyfriend doesn't deserve husband benefits. Example: Both parties want marriage, friends with benefits or a short-term relationship! You and your love interest always need to be on the same page. Never take it personally or as a loss because men are like buses; there is always one behind the next.

4. Pay attention to the time: Notice if you're dating someone and they are not adding you to their life currently. If they have "I" plans instead of "we" plans they are not focusing on making a future with you and adding value to your life. They might not be ready to be with you. Learn from my mistakes

now so that your future won't be a repeat of your past.

5. You can appreciate but do not compensate (date smart): Allow the person to grow into the person they need to become. If not let them go. Never allow complacency. You are valuable.

6. Do not expect anyone to love you more than you love yourself: Your peace and happiness come from you and not anyone else. If you're single, work while you wait. Keep your standards, become the love that you truly want to attract. Pray, and God will give you the desires of your heart.

6. Never take your CROWN off: Do not ever lower your standards because you only go through what you allow. Queens, do not keep a man around just for the company because of loneliness and desperation. Beware there are some men out in the

world who will date women just to lower her standards to uplift his ego. You should never compromise your self-worth for love because pain is not loved. Love can be disguised as self-hate; please pray and discern that spirit. If you want that man but he is not doing the right thing, "LET HIM GO so that HE CAN GROW." Sometimes the only way someone will learn how to appreciate you is in your absence, not in your presence.

Real love

(1 Corinthians 13:4) Love is patient; love is kind. It does not envy, it does not boast, it is not proud. It is not rude, it is not self-seeking, it is not easily angered, it keeps no record of wrongs. Love does not delight in evil but rejoices with the truth. It

always protects, always trusts, always hope, always perseveres. Love never fails.

Don't let anyone tell you that real love doesn't exist. I see it daily and feel it daily. It's limitless, unconditional, everlasting, forgiving, patient, giving and kind. It loves me more than I could ever love myself. Love gave its only begotten son for my sins so that I can live. Love wakes me up every day. Love orders my steps. Love forgives me of my sins. Love keeps me whole and in perfect peace. Love never fails. Love teaches me how to love others even when I don't know how. So love didn't hurt you, someone who didn't know how to love hurt you. Love doesn't hurt people; hurt people, hurt people. So please know that pain isn't to love, because GOD is love and God loves YOU.

I hope this book blessed you and if it did, please share it with your sisters, daughters, and friends. Thank you so much, and I LOVE YOU!

ABOUT THE AUTHOR

Candra Jones is a Confidence Coach, Motivational Speaker, Success Strategist, Author, and Visionary. She is the Founder and CEO of Glamorous Beauty Essentials LLC, and she serves as the Executive Director of the Girls ENpower Movement. She devotes herself to empowering people to achieve spiritual growth, personal transformation by unlocking their confidence and being authentic in their power so that they can reach their full potential in life. Candra creates and delivers products and services such as conferences, seminars, workshops, brunches and training that are designed for millennial entrepreneurial women on both national and international platforms. Her life motto is: Live in your Greatness

Make your next event successful!

Book Candra Jones to speak

Contact Information

http://www.candrajones.com

info@candrajones.com